31 PRAYERS FOR MY Daughter

Aaron & Jennifer Smith

31 PRAYERS FOR MY DAUGHTER
Seeking God's Perfect Will for Her

Written By Aaron & Jennifer Smith

Cover By Ciera Rose - Cierarose.com

Interior Format & Layout By Miles Albritton

ISBN-10: 0-9863667-9-X

ISBN-13: 978-0-9863667-9-6

LCCN: 2017916503

31prayersformydaughter.com

Printed in U.S.A

CONTENTS

Cry Out In The Night

"Arise, cry out in the night,
at the beginning of the night watches!
Pour out your heart like water
before the presence of the Lord!
Lift your hands to him
for the lives of your children"

Lamentations 2:19

INTRODUCTION

The lily is a tall, slender perennial, with a large, prominent flower. A lily is fragrant, its petals are soft, and its colors are vibrant. The blooms of a lily are magnificent, graceful in stature, evidence of God's creative handiwork. This flower is a true gift.

Likewise, your daughter is a true gift from God. His creative design is evident in her life. The details that make her unique were intentional and thoughtful. Her colorful character reflects beauty as she blooms and matures into womanhood. She is soft; she is feminine, she is fragile like a flower. She is your daughter, and it's good to celebrate who she is, who God created her to be.

You were used by God to plant a seed, and that seed is your sweet daughter. You are responsible for nurturing her as she grows, tending to her needs, watering her with the Word, praying for her and with her, and loving her unconditionally. You are a significant and essential part of her life.

"Train up a child in the way he should go;
   even when he is old he will not depart from it." Proverbs
22:6

Becoming a parent is truly a miraculous and incomparable experience. Being able to look into your child's eyes and immediately know, without a doubt, you have a significant purpose in their life, is unparalleled and pure. God, in His infinite wisdom, created and established "family," a necessary and vital component of every society.

Life is precious to God, and in His goodness, He has entrusted you to protect life, to cultivate love in your family, so that life can thrive and the legacy of love can be passed down to the next generations.

Children are, and children will always be an extraordinary blessing.

Your perspective and your heart toward children should resemble that of Christ...and He exemplified a heart for children.

"Then children were brought to him that he might lay his hands on them and pray. The disciples rebuked the people, but Jesus said, "Let the little children come to me and do not hinder them, for to such belongs the kingdom of heaven." And he laid his hands on them and went away." Matthew 19:13-14

God has entrusted you with your daughter. Not only is it a huge blessing for you to be a significant part of her life, but in addition to that, you are doing important work in your daughter's life. You are influencing her and training her up to be the woman God has created her to be. Every day you get to spend with her, you are discipling her heart, teaching her about God, and setting the foundation for her future. This work happens every single day with every choice you make. There is no substitute, and there is no replacement for who you are in your daughter's life. Being a parent will seldom be easy or convenient, but it is worth it.

When your days get tough, remember that it is not your spouse or your children who are the enemy. You have a real enemy, and he is trying as hard as he can to destroy your family. He wants to devour your children. You must be prepared to fight for your family. You must be willing to enter into the battlefield, which is prayer.

Prayer is crucial. You must be eager and diligent to pray every day for your daughter. As you take the time to pray for your daughter, you will consider her greatest needs, petitioning God to help her. Prayer is an awesome way to offer thanksgiving to God for your daughter, and it is also a powerful way to defend against the enemy. As you faithfully purpose to pray for your daughter, you will inevitably experience intimacy with God. How beautiful it is to know that by praying for your daughter, you are embracing a relationship with God and pursuing intimacy with Him!

My husband and I can personally testify to the power of prayer, which is why we agree with the Bible and strongly encourage others to have a heart dedicated to prayer. I truly believe our marriage has been saved because of my husband's obedience to pray every day. When our relationship was enduring hardship, and we almost gave up, it was prayer that reminded us to be thankful, hopeful, and to endure. It was the humility required to approach God for help that gave us the perspective needed to hang on to what we had. God heard our prayers and was faithful to help us.

Through our online ministries for husbands and wives (Husband Revolution & Unveiled Wife), we wanted to encourage these couples with a resource that promoted the very thing that helped us, motivating us to write Thirty-One Prayers For My Wife and Thirty-One Prayers For My Husband. The feedback we have received from couples taking our 31 Prayer Challenge has been astounding. Testimonies continue to flood in from husbands and wives about how God is moving in their hearts and marriages.

We praise God for the breakthroughs marriages are experiencing because of these resources.

We desire to be great parents, but we are also in a season of learning through experience. In our insecurities about parenting, being bombarded by fears and doubts, we call out to God and rely on Him and His Word to guide us as parents. God has been faithful to help us and walk with us through our parenting journey.

We wrote this book because we want to help you and motivate you to pray for your daughter or daughters. Most of all we want you to draw closer to God through the power of prayer!

This resource is not a magical book that will solve your parenting questions, nor will praying these prayers guarantee that you will have a perfect child. However, the Bible is clear that we are to come to God and submit everything to Him in prayer.

"Do not be anxious about anything, but in everything by prayer and supplication with thanksgiving let your requests be made known to God." - Philippians 4:6 ESV

Praying for your daughter's life will remind your heart not to worry, but rather trust in God and His timing for everything.

As you submit your heart to God in obedient prayer, you will see Him move! And oh how wonderful it will be to one day hear a testimony from your daughter about how your prayers helped her! You can read these prayers straight from the text, you can say them out loud, you can get on your knees, or stand with your hands raised up toward the sky.

Please understand that we wrote this book in a such a way that it is relevant for every daughter, regardless of age. These prayers could easily be for a 3-month-old, as it could for a 3-year-old, even as it could for a 13-year-old. If there is a prayer that doesn't quite cover exactly what you are experiencing with your daughter we encourage you to make the prayer more personal by adding to it using the journal lines provided.

Remember she is God's daughter, and He is going to be blessed knowing you care so much for her that you are willing to make the time to pray for her heart!

**We have included a few challenges to encourage you to consider the significance and purpose of praying for your daughter. There is a total of 7 challenges. We urge you to pray about each one and then fulfill it as the Lord leads you.*

***We would also love to see your journey along the way! Update your social media and tag @unveiledwife and @ husbandrevolution #PrayersForMyDaughter so we can follow along and see how God is moving in your life, as well as in the lives of your children!*

Our Prayer For You

Dear Heavenly Father,

Thank You for the parent reading this book. Thank You for the gift and blessing of their child. May You bless this family in great big beautiful ways. May Your Holy Spirit lead this family ever closer to You. May these prayers be used as a guide to bless, encourage, and anoint their precious daughter as they petition for her heart and pray that one day she receives Your gift of salvation. May these prayers be used to bring this family closer to You, closer together, stronger, and more full of love than ever before.

In Jesus' name, AMEN!

A Prayer For The Parent

Praying for your daughter is an honorable thing to do. Throughout this book, you will be praying for specific parts of her life and her future. As much as this is a huge initiative and selfless way of loving her, please don't skip over the importance of praying for your heart and journey as her parent. Please devote time to praying and asking God to help you be the parent He created you to be. This prayer is for you. Pray it as many times as you desire and add to it the areas of parenting you desire more wisdom and help from your Heavenly Father. He is faithful to encourage and equip you. Pray and listen. Then persevere.

Dear Heavenly Father,

Thank You for giving me the opportunity to be a parent. Thank You for trusting me with my daughter. Thank You for the relationship that we have. I pray we both would treasure our relationship. Show me how to parent her well. Teach me Your ways, O Lord. Help me to navigate Your Word and to use it as my foundation for parenting. I pray my relationship with You would be a beautiful example for my daughter. I pray she would come to know You through me. Send people into my life who have experience with parenting, who live according to Your Word, and who can help guide me. I pray You would give me eyes to truly see my daughter. Give me a compassionate heart toward her, especially when she is having a difficult day. I pray my words are gentle and my actions reaffirm my love for her. Please help me to say the hard things when I need to. I pray I never shy away from leading my daughter as You need me and have called me to do. I pray I would be a patient parent, quick to listen, and quick to apologize when I sin against her. God, may nothing separate my love for my daughter. May nothing ever come between us that severs intimacy. I pray we always have open communication and trust. Most of all, may You be glorified in my parenting and my relationship with my daughter.

In Jesus' name, AMEN!

DAY 1
A Blessing For Her

Isaiah 54:13

Dear Lord,

Thank You for the gift of my daughter. She is delightful and beautiful. She has been created in Your image and with great purpose. I pray You would use me to teach her Your ways and reveal Yourself to her. I pray You and her would have an extraordinary relationship. I pray she never doubts Your love for her. I pray she is never confused about why You created her. Do not let any voices of doubt find room in her heart. Give my daughter confidence in You. I pray my daughter grows into an honorable woman. I pray my daughter is kind and respectful to all. I pray she stands for truth and defends Your Word. I pray she strives for righteousness. Give her an understanding of forgiveness and grace. Remove any selfish ways, any sin that entangles her. I pray against the enemy and his desire to tear her down. Be a shield and a tower of refuge for my daughter. Uphold her with Your righteous right hand. Bless my daughter with confidence and purity. Bless my daughter with an unexplainable joy that radiates from her heart all the days of her life. Bless my daughter with an amazing immune system. Bless her with endurance as she faces trials and tribulation. Bless my daughter with wisdom that is evident in her every word and action. Bless her with good friends who care deeply about her. Bless her with a husband who cherishes her. Bless her with children she can nurture and raise to know You. I pray my daughter sees the blessings You have lavished her with and may her heart be grateful. Lord, please bless my daughter with Your peace that surpasses all understanding.

In Jesus' name, AMEN!

PERSONALIZE

Use this area to write a personalized prayer for your Daughter. You can also write a list of things you would like to continue to pray for.

CHALLENGE

- #1 -

Start a Prayer Journal

Start a prayer journal: Start a prayer journal that you will one day gift to your child when she is older. Use this journal to write down your prayers, specifically for your daughter. Give it to her as a gift for a milestone celebration such as her baptism, her graduation, her wedding, or when she becomes a mother.

DAY 2

Salvation

Romans 10:9-10

Dear Lord,

Thank You for my daughter's life. Thank You for loving her and thank You for letting me be her parent. Thank You for being her good Father. Thank You for loving her so much that You would rescue her from sin by sending Jesus Christ as a sacrifice, that she may have eternal life with You. I pray my daughter would grasp the magnitude of Your love for her. I pray she understands just how deep and how wide Your love is. I pray my daughter would receive Salvation and the gift of grace You freely give. I pray my daughter would have open eyes to see her sin and her need for You. I pray she would have a heart of repentance. I pray she would believe in Jesus Christ, that You raised Him from the dead, and I pray she confesses with her mouth that He is Lord. Sanctify her. Transform her. Please bless my daughter with wisdom so that she understands what it means to be reconciled to You and that she walks in victory over sin. I pray she would fear You her whole life. I pray nothing would be a greater priority than her relationship with You. Lord, please help her to be open and honest with You. I pray she would be intimate with You, sharing the deepest parts of her heart with You. May she remain hopeful throughout her life, no matter what circumstances she faces, knowing confidently that her salvation means eternity with You. May she look forward to heaven. I pray her salvation in You would be a catalyst for extraordinary endeavors in her life. I pray she is motivated to share Your love with others in hopes of bringing salvation to the lives of others.

In Jesus' name, AMEN!

PERSONALIZE

Use this area to write a personalized prayer for your Daughter. You can also write a list of things you would like to continue to pray for.

DAY 3

Purity

Matthew 5:8

Dear Lord,

I pray my daughter would strive to live a pure life. I pray her speech would be pure. I pray she would save herself for marriage and that in her marriage she continues to live purely. I pray she would have eyes to identify what things are pure and what are not pure. When she chooses music, movies, or any other form of entertainment that she filters it, only allowing herself to experience what is pure. Please help her to understand purity is power. Reveal to her the beauty in purity. I also pray she recognizes how living a pure life protects life. Show her in Your Word why purity is important. Send influences into her life that will support her in staying pure, because they also strive to be pure. Lord, I pray my daughter would feel confident as she walks in purity. I pray she is blessed because she is pure in heart. I pray she sees You clearly because she is pure in heart. Help her to guard herself against the temptation to be impure. May Your Holy Word guide her and be her sword to defend her purity. I pray no person ever takes advantage of her. I pray no evil finds its way into her heart. I pray against the schemes of the enemy who seeks to destroy her purity. I pray my daughter has the self-control to abstain from immorality. Strengthen her and give her peace. Create in her a clean heart, O Lord. I pray my daughter is an advocate for purity in this self-gratifying culture. May her light shine bright and may she encourage others to live a life of purity.

In Jesus' name, AMEN!

DAY 4

Her Identity

Genesis 1:27

Dear Lord,

I pray You would reveal to my daughter Your purpose for her life. I pray she would comprehend the truth that You created her in Your image. I pray she would see how precious she is to You and to me. I pray she would never wrestle with her identity. I pray she would never doubt Your thoughtful design of her. I pray she would know You planned every detail of what makes her, uniquely her. I pray she would celebrate her life, who she is in You, and how You intentionally created her. I pray my daughter is not deceived about her gender identity and sexual identity. I pray my daughter is never confused about what to believe to be the truth about her identity. I pray she confidently knows her identity is wrapped up in You. I pray she embraces being a female. I pray she embraces her body and how You created it. I pray she embraces having been made in Your image. Help her to see what a great and marvelous thing it is to be made in Your image. I pray she embraces Your Word as truth and lives according to it. May You protect my daughter from any confusing messages about identity the enemy might try to use to draw her away from You. I pray she is never a victim of labels. Equip her to know Your truth. Use me to teach her Your truth and to affirm her identity. If she does wrestle with her identity, I pray she discovers her identity in Your Holy Word. I pray my daughter would find peace in identifying with Christ. As an image bearer, I pray she would represent Your truth to the world. I pray others would see how confident she is in her identity and ask her what she stands for. I pray she would be like seasoned salt, helping others to taste and see that You are good.

In Jesus' name, AMEN!

CHALLENGE

- #2 -

Consider This

Consider the thoughtfulness God poured into creating your daughter and making her in His image. Think about her unique character and her vast abilities. Take time to thank God for her. Then take a moment to share with your daughter all of the incredible things you considered about her.

DAY 5

Her Beauty

1 Peter 3:3-4

Dear Lord,

There is an abundance of beauty in Your creation. The world is full of Your incredible handiwork. Although there are many things that radiate Your beauty, I see it most in people. Thank You for my beautiful daughter. Thank You for every detail You intentionally put into making my daughter. I pray my daughter sees how beautiful she is, inside and out. Reveal to her the goodness in her character. Give her an elevated perspective so that she may see her strengths and abilities. I desire my daughter to know what she is capable of. I pray she never fears failure. I pray she is never paralyzed by other people's negative opinions. Send people into her life who will speak positively to her. May they encourage her by affirming the beauty they see in her. I pray my daughter would believe the truth about herself and dwell on those truths. I pray against voices of condemnation. I pray against voices of insecurity and doubt. I pray my daughter would be a confident woman. Help her to know her value and worth. I pray she wouldn't rely on the love of men to make her feel valued. I pray she wouldn't rely on approval from others to validate her worth. I pray she wouldn't rely on material things, immodest clothing or expensive fashion to affirm her beauty. I pray my daughter lets Your opinion of her be enough. I pray she relies on You to validate her worth. I pray she has faith to accept Your love and let it satisfy her completely. Thank You for my beautiful daughter. Use me, O Lord, to remind her daily of her worth.

In Jesus' name, AMEN!

DAY 6

Wisdom

Proverbs 1:7

Dear Lord,

I pray my daughter would be full of wisdom. I pray throughout her life she continues to grow in understanding of who You are. Bless my daughter with wisdom and knowledge. I pray she fears You with a reverent heart. I pray she tests everything according to Your Word, that she may know what is true and what Your perfect will is for her life. I pray she has a desire to read Your Word. I have faith that she will follow You with her whole heart and that she will live in submission to You. I pray she has a heart of obedience to all that You command. I pray she would mature into a wise woman who is willing to teach others who You are. I pray she applies wisdom in her every response. I pray wisdom preserves my daughter's life, saving her from the threat of painful circumstances. Holy Spirit, convict my daughter to walk in the Spirit. Give her a desire to learn every day of her life. I pray she is humble and teachable. I pray she allows others to help her grow. I pray my daughter has amazing comprehension, that she is a quick learner, and that she applies the knowledge she receives. Like a deep well that satisfies the thirst of a community, may my daughter bless those around her with the wisdom she has acquired. May she be a well of good news and peace, an ambassador eager to share Your Gospel with others. Bless my daughter with an abundance of wisdom and may she use it to glorify You.

In Jesus' name, AMEN!

Being a G

Parent

Being a parent is never convenient and your flesh will fight it. Yet, it is one of the most worthy things you will ever experience. Die to your flesh daily. Walk in the Spirit.

DAY 1

Peace

Philippians 4:4-7

Dear Lord,

In a day and age where there is so much evil and unrest, I pray my daughter has extraordinary peace. Please protect her from the evil in this world. May Your peace rest upon her right now. I pray she is never overwhelmed by anxious thoughts. May peace abound in her heart and mind. At the first hint of anxiety, may she come to You for comfort. I pray her first response is always prayer. Teach her how to pray. May I be an example to her of how to live a life of praying without ceasing. When she is in the midst of storms that are raging and threatening her sense of security, may she remember that You are with her. Holy Spirit, please counsel my daughter and help her navigate the roughness of any and every storm. I pray when conflict overwhelms her heart that Your Word would gently guide her through it. I pray against bad sleep and bad dreams. May You protect her mind as she lays down to rest. Help her to relax. I pray against fearful thoughts. May Your peace bring rest to her soul. Refresh my daughter, that she may feel equipped to endure what she encounters each and every day. I pray the peace my daughter has is an encouragement to others around her. May they be comforted by You through my daughter. I pray she is a vessel of Your peace, pouring it out generously to all. When life gets loud and busy, help my daughter to slow down and seek quietness and stillness in Your presence.

In Jesus' name, AMEN!

DAY 8

A Servant Heart

Galatians 5:13

Dear Lord,

Jesus Christ came, and He served with a humble heart. I pray my daughter serves with a humble heart. I pray her motivation is the same as Christ's, Your pure love. I pray my daughter has a servant heart, willing and ready to serve at all times. I pray she doesn't grumble or complain when she is asked to help. May she be quick to respond with a joyful attitude. May she see it as an opportunity to serve You, her almighty King. I also pray she serves thoughtfully, without being asked or prompted. May she initiate serving others in creative ways. I pray her love for serving others reaps an intrinsic value for her. I pray she never serves for selfish gain and may she never expect anything in return. I pray You would strengthen her when she goes through seasons of constant serving. I pray You would sustain her so that she is capable of handling much. Lord, I pray my daughter would find joy in serving her family. May she find beauty in being a helping hand, a shoulder to lean on, and comforting arms to embrace. May she be ready to share Your encouraging words with others at the exact time You need her to speak Your truth. May she have eyes to see when others are in need and may she know how to be helpful in those times. I pray against the temptation to be selfish or doing things only for personal gain. I pray my daughter is selfless. I pray she puts others first just as Christ has done for us. Bless her, O Lord.

In Jesus' name, AMEN!

CHALLENGE

- #3 -

Write God a Letter

Share with Him your whole heart, your hopes
and fears about parenting, and what you are
currently feeling or experiencing.

DAY 9

Contentment

Philippians 4:12-13

Dear Lord,

Thank You for Your provision. You are so good, and Your faithfulness is everlasting. Thank You for my daughter whom I love with my whole heart. I pray my daughter would know that You have generously provided for her and continue to do so. I pray she recognizes the incredible gifts You have lavished her with. I pray my daughter would be content, no matter her circumstances. I pray she would understand that whether she has a lot of food or a little, whether she has many clothes or just a few, whether she has more than enough wealth or no wealth at all, may she be able to call You Lord of her life. I pray she accepts what You have for her. I pray she recognizes the differences between desire and necessity. May she come to You in prayer with her requests, having faith You will be her provider. I pray she trusts in You for everything. I pray her hope never fails. I pray her relationship with You is not dependent on how much You give her. I pray she would love You and trust You regardless of what You provide or choose not to provide. Help her to be a good steward with all that you do give to her. I pray I would be a good example to my daughter by being content. Help my daughter to know the secret to being content in every situation. May happiness be evident by the smile that glows on her face. May her heart be satisfied all the days of her life. May her contentment in life bring glory to Your name.

In Jesus' name, AMEN!

DAY 10

Embracing Modesty

1 Corinthians 6:19-20

Dear Lord,

Thank You for my daughter. I pray she grasps the significance of her body being a holy temple for Your Holy Spirit to dwell in. I pray she understands the responsibility she has in caring for her body and using it appropriately. Help her to know the influence she has in the lives of others through the way she talks, her body language, and how she dresses. I pray she strives to protect herself from the eyes of lustful people by intentionally covering the parts of her body that should be reserved for her and her husband only. I pray my daughter would embrace modesty. I pray she would live with a conviction that compels her to have decency in her behavior. Help her to comprehend the value of modesty. I pray she would never use immodesty as a means to feel valued or validated. May she never be convinced that immodesty leads to true love. Rather, I pray my daughter confidently knows her worth, knows that she is beautiful, knows that she is loved and cherished by You. I pray against the temptation of immodesty. I pray against any and all lies that beauty is found in immodest behavior, speech, or dress. Raise up my daughter to share the truth with her friends and other women, that they are made in God's image and are already valuable in His eyes, and that modesty is beautiful and respectable. I pray my daughter embraces Your love for her.

In Jesus' name, AMEN!

DAY 11
Pursuing God

Proverbs 8:17

Dear Lord,

Thank You for this beautiful day. Thank You for my family. Thank You for the gift of my precious daughter. I feel so blessed to be a significant part of her life. Thank You for trusting me with her. I pray our relationship continues to grow. I pray I can teach her how to pursue You. I pray she knows You because of my relationship with You. I pray her heart turns toward You and that she receives You as her Lord and Savior. I pray she seeks after You every day. I pray she reads Your Word and studies it. I pray You would surround her with people who also love Your Word and live by it. In a world that does not honor You and celebrates immorality, I pray she stands steadfast and strong according to Your Word. I pray nothing would steal her joy. I pray You would guard her heart against deceitfulness. Help her to discern Your truth. I pray she finds time to read your Holy Word every single day. I pray she spends time meditating on it and memorizing it. Write it on the tablet of her heart. I pray it is Your Word that guides her through life. May she run to Your Word always, especially in times of need, times of hardship, and times of thankfulness. I pray my daughter praises You, O Lord. I pray she spends time listening to You as well. I pray she never wrestles with doubt or insecurity in her relationship with You. I pray my daughter submits her life to You. I pray she submits to You every desire she has and every plan she sets out to do. I pray she relies on You and trusts You for all of her needs as she pursues You and pursues her purpose in You!

In Jesus' name, AMEN!

The S

Exa

eatest

mple

The greatest example of love you can show your child is the way you love your spouse. Let your marriage be the reason she desires to get married one day.

DAY 12

Gentleness

Ephesians 4:1-3

Dear Lord,

I pray my daughter is full of gentleness. I pray she is gentle with her every word and her every action. I pray gentleness is an attribute other people admire in her. I pray her gentleness would bless her family and friends. I pray it would inspire others to be gentle. I also pray she is kind and gentle in ways that encourage and uplift those around her. Lord, I pray my daughter is gentle with children. I pray she loves children and enjoys their company. I pray she is always quick to serve mothers who are in need of a little extra help. I pray my daughter has a desire to be a mother. Use my daughter to bless the little children in her life. I pray her relationship with children is a source of great joy. I pray my daughter would be a woman of great patience. May she bear with one another in love, eager to maintain the unity of peace with everyone as much as it is in her power to do so. I pray my daughter is affectionate with a gentle touch, giving people hugs and showing them through physical touch that they are loved. I pray that when she becomes a wife, she would be gentle in her responses toward her husband. Encourage her to be thoughtful of others and to put their needs above her own. I pray her words would be drawn up from her heart and delivered with utmost gentleness that those who receive her words are blessed. Thank You for my daughter and thank You for giving her the gift of gentleness.

In Jesus' name, AMEN!

DAY 13

Her Attitude

Philippians 2:14-15

Dear Lord,

I lift up my sweet daughter to You today. I pray You would bless her and overwhelm her with Your presence, reminding her that You are near to her. Remind her that she is greatly loved. If there is anything in her life right now causing her physical pain or emotional pain, please help her through it. Be her strength so she may persevere. Reconcile any relationships out of order. Build her up so that she can withstand even the most difficult challenges. Right now, I specifically pray for my daughter's attitude. I pray her behavior reflects a deep trust in You. May she be someone who is full of joy, slow to be angered, and quick to be thankful. I pray her attitude is always one that reflects Christ's character. May the posture of her heart be humble and kind. Whatever she does throughout her life, I pray she does it without grumbling or complaint. I pray my daughter would be respectful, especially to authority. I pray she treats elderly people with dignity. May her appreciation and love for people be motivated by Your love. Help her to consider others more important than herself, and to seek their interests above her own. I pray my daughter would shine bright in this dark world. I pray against the temptation to act out negatively because of circumstances. Help my daughter to be a stable woman who operates in self-control. Help her to learn self-control over her emotions. I pray she can express and communicate her feelings in a respectful way. Bless my daughter with a humble and righteous attitude that adds to both her inner and outward beauty.

In Jesus' name, AMEN!

CHALLENGE

- #4 -

Write a Response

Write a response to your letter to God, from God's perspective. What do you think He would say to encourage you?

DAY 14

Understanding Joy

James 1:2-4

Dear Lord,

Please continue to build a firm foundation for my daughter's life, that she may grow into the faithful woman You created her to be. I pray Your Word increases her faith, reinforcing the pillars of truth that will help her navigate this life. Use me, O Lord, to bless my daughter, to train her up in the way she should go, and to show her what true love is. I pray You would be magnified in her life. I pray You would give my daughter a profound understanding of joy. Bless her with an abundance of joy overflowing from her heart at all times. May her face reflect the joy that resides in her heart. I pray I model for my daughter the power of pure joy. I pray we experience laughter together. I pray we can face tough times together, with joy keeping us stable in all our ways. Even when there is conflict in our relationship or tears from other painful circumstances, please help us to remain faithful, hopeful, and joyful until our hearts are reconciled. I pray my daughter clings to joy through the various trials that she faces so that the testing of her faith produces steadfastness. Mature her, O Lord, and may she be perfect and complete, lacking in nothing. May her joy be evidence to all that You are her source of joy and strength. May her face reflect the confidence and faith she has in You so that others are blessed by her countenance.

In Jesus' name, AMEN!

DAY 15
Fruit Of The Spirit

Galatians 5:22-23

Dear Lord,

Thank You for the fruit of the Spirit. Thank You for revealing such incredible attributes we produce as we abide in You. I pray my daughter abides in You, Lord. I pray Your Word falls on the rich soil of her heart, growing and producing the fruit of Your Spirit. I pray that in all her ways she expresses love, joy, peace, patience, kindness, goodness, faithfulness, gentleness, and self-control. May this fruit be ever growing, luscious, and abundant in her life. I pray others would see this evidence and know that it is a byproduct and result of following You. I pray this fruit blesses others richly. I pray others would experience this fruit in my daughter's life, tasting and seeing that You are good. May I abide in You that this fruit may be abundant in my life as well. I pray my daughter gets to receive the blessing of having a loving, joyful, peaceful, patient, kind, good, faithful, gentle, and self-controlled parent to nurture her and bless her all the days of her life. I pray this fruit produced in my life would contribute to a healthy home environment. I pray this fruit would cultivate a safe place for my daughter to open up and be honest with me. I pray we would share an extraordinary relationship with each other, where trust resides. Break down any walls between us, hindering us from connecting. I pray I would be a good listener for my daughter, that I would slow down and be present with her. May Your Holy Spirit water our hearts and cultivate in us the character of Christ.

In Jesus' name, AMEN!

DAY 16

Her Purpose

Psalm 138:8

Dear Lord,

You are so amazing! Your love endures forever! Thank You for my daughter. I pray my daughter would confidently know You created her with purpose. Reveal to her what Your purpose is for her life. I pray You would use her to impact people's lives for Your Kingdom. Use her to turn hearts toward You. I pray the desire to do extraordinary things would swell up in her heart. Spark in my daughter's mind inspiration and creativity for how she can fulfill Your perfect will. Reveal to her what You are loading up in her tool belt and what resources You are giving her to fulfill her purpose. I also pray that as she operates within her giftings and fulfills Your will that she recognizes Your hand in her life. Guide her and direct her as she makes pivotal decisions in her life. I pray she shares details of these decisions with me and trusts me to help her figure out the way she should go. May Your Holy Spirit speak to her and lead her to do great and mighty works. As she does these works for You, may she also give You all the glory. I pray there is no work too big that intimidates her and no work too small that seems unnecessary. Show her the value in it all. I pray pride never gets in the way of what You desire to do with her life. May she never have a lack of vision for her life or wrestle with what her purpose is. Make it clear to her, Lord. I pray she would believe in her heart that You intentionally created her with purpose and that she would seek to fulfill that purpose all the days of her life.

In Jesus' name, AMEN!

DAY 17

Love & Romance

Song of Solomon 6:3

Dear Lord,

You never hesitate to love us in profound ways. You love us in personal ways. You love us in extraordinary ways. I pray Your love would captivate my daughter. Call her by name and draw her close to Yourself. Woo her with the magnificent colors of sunsets, the delicate design of flowers, the vast expanse of the stars, and the coolness of the breeze. Let all of the things You have created be evidence of Your great love for her. I pray Your scriptures give her comfort and clarity in times of need. I also pray the love she receives from others would be affirmations of how wide and deep Your love for her truly is. Thank You for loving my daughter. I pray Your love continues to impact her life and transform her. Thank You for showing her how to love. I pray I would also be an example to my daughter of how to love well. Holy Spirit, please empower me and equip me to love her unconditionally. Lord, I ask You give my daughter a correct perspective of true love. I pray she never uses manipulation as a means of gaining more love. May Your love satisfy her. I pray her love is pure. I pray she has a desire for marriage and that she would love her husband. Help her to understand love is not just a feeling, but a choice she gets to make every day. I pray her marriage relationship is beautiful. I pray she experiences romance and adventure with her husband. I pray they love each other deeply and that their love satisfies each other. May their love be a reflection to others of Your amazing love story.

In Jesus' name, AMEN!

Discip

the

You are responsible for discipling the heart of your child. Teach her God's ways by walking with integrity every single day.

DAY 18

Her Education

Proverbs 18:15

Dear Lord,

Thank You for the gift of education. Thank You for Your provision so that my daughter can be educated. Help my daughter and me to communicate clearly as we navigate the learning process together. I pray You would equip me to confidently teach my daughter. Help me to take advantage of all the little ways I can teach her throughout life that will impact her and help her on her educational journey. My daughter has access to an immense amount of rich knowledge. Open her eyes and her heart that she may recognize the access she has to gain knowledge and may she appreciate it. I pray my daughter has a hunger for knowledge. Motivate her heart to be a person who seeks after learning. I pray she uses every opportunity You give to her to grow and mature through learning. I pray my daughter values education. I pray she understands how to use the knowledge You give to her. If the purpose and passion You give her leads her to a need of higher education, may You also provide the means for her to remain debt free. I pray my daughter keeps her education as a significant priority in her life. I pray she excels in school. I pray she respects any and all who teach her. I pray she would never feel pressured or stressed because of school, rather may she be motivated to do good and learn through experience. May You mature her emotionally, mentally, physically, and spiritually. May she use her education to glorify You.

In Jesus' name, AMEN!

DAY 19

Prayer Warrior

Philippians 4:6

Dear Lord,

Your Word says to pray without ceasing. I pray my daughter has a heart that is quick to pray. No matter what circumstances or situations are taking place in her life, may she always be thoughtful to pray first. May she have a heart of gratitude, thanking You for all of the good gifts in her life. May she also be willing to thank You for the challenges You allow her to face, knowing they will produce in her perseverance. May she seek Your face daily. May she humble herself by kneeling before Your Holy throne. I pray my daughter is willing to be intimate with You, sharing with You the deepest parts of her heart. I pray she understands the value of prayer. I pray she guards her time with You. I pray my daughter is a prayer warrior, warring for the hearts of her family and friends, petitioning to You for their salvation. I pray my daughter seeks after You like a best friend. I pray my daughter loves You and I pray she takes time to listen to You. Speak to my daughter. Reveal mighty things to her about who You are, what You are doing in the world, and about what the future holds. As she surrenders her heart to You through prayer, please transform her. Mold her and shape her just as a potter molds the clay, that she would be a vessel used for Your glory. I pray my daughter wouldn't hesitate to pray for her health, for circumstances she endures, for her friends, for even strangers she meets. I pray her heart is humbled through prayer.

In Jesus' name, AMEN!

CHALLENGE

- #5 -

The Most Important Thing

Salvation is the most important thing. Spend time kneeling in prayer, petitioning on behalf of your daughter, praying that she accepts Jesus Christ as her personal Lord and Savior and that she spends her life seeking after God wholeheartedly.

DAY 20

A Generous Heart

Luke 6:38

Dear Lord,

You are generous. Your provision is never lacking. I pray my daughter would have a generous heart. I pray she recognizes that everything she has, was given to her by You. I pray she holds money and material possessions loosely. Teach her how to steward well everything You give to her. When needs are made apparent in other people's lives, I pray she would be quick to help where she can to meet those needs. I pray against pride and selfishness. I pray against the temptation to grip onto things for herself. I pray against thoughts of fairness and jealousy. Help my daughter to walk in the Spirit and to give as generously as You have. I pray I can give generously to my daughter. Help me today to find a way to provide for one of her needs. Give me eyes to see the needs of my daughter. Holy Spirit, prompt my heart to give to my daughter what You want her to have. I pray my daughter and I would spend time together to consider different ways of blessing others in our local community. May Your provision for others flow through our family. I pray my daughter would understand through first-hand experience that it truly is better to give than to receive. May generosity be a gift she carries with her throughout her lifetime. May others come to salvation in You through my daughter's willingness to be generous. I pray she is willing to share what she has with family and friends with a good attitude.

In Jesus' name, AMEN!

DAY 21

Her Health

3 John 1:2

Dear Lord,

I lift up my daughter's health to You today. I pray she would have a strong immune system. Give her strength and endurance. Give her a sound mind that can think clearly with keen focus. I pray my daughter's body makes her feel young and vibrant. I pray she chooses to eat well. Help her to understand that food is fuel for her body. Help her also not to be a picky eater. I pray against the temptation to eat food that is not healthy and I pray against the temptation to overeat. Help my daughter to keep a balanced diet that will nourish her body. Help me to be a good example to her when it comes to having a healthy self-image and a healthy relationship with food. I pray against any sickness or illness that tries to threaten her body. Remove any inflammation or tenderness. If anything aches or hurts, please heal her immediately. I pray my daughter is proactive in staying healthy. Please motivate her to exercise. I pray my daughter engages her muscles and appreciates the ability she has to move her body. I pray she stays strong by working out so that she can keep up with the demands of everyday life. I pray she enjoys working out. Terminate any ounce of laziness she may have. I pray the knowledge she receives about having good health is applied through wisdom. I pray her mind is healthy; I pray her heart is healthy, I pray her relationship with You is healthy. Thank You, Lord for my daughter's health.

In Jesus' name, AMEN!

DAY 11

The Word

Hebrews 4:12

Dear Lord,

Thank You for the gift of Your Holy Word. Your Word is living truth. It is active, and it acts as a helper and a guide. Your Word is transforming. Thank You for making Your Word available. I pray You would help me to encourage my daughter to read You Word every day. I pray my daughter has an insatiable desire to read Your Holy Word. I pray Your Word is a lamp for her feet and a manual for how she lives. Your Word comforts and corrects. Your Word is how You speak to my daughter. I pray my daughter allows Your Word to sink into her heart. I pray she allows Your Word to discern her thoughts and intentions. May Your Word pierce her heart and transform her character. I pray she makes reading Your Word a priority in her life. I pray she understands Your Word. I pray she knows that Your Word is powerful and can transform her life. May she never be intimidated by Your Word. Help her to navigate Your Word with wisdom. I pray she enjoys reading it. I pray my daughter stands boldly for Your truth. I pray she is unwavering, stable, and courageous. I pray my daughter fights for Your truth. I pray she is never deceived by the enemy or by culture's agenda. I pray she is quick to use the Word as a sword to fight against evil. I pray Your Words are written on her heart. If anyone ever asks her why she believes what she does, may she help them navigate Your scripture. Equip me to know Your Word so that I can use it to encourage my daughter.

In Jesus' name, AMEN!

DAY 23

Exercising Self-control

2 Timothy 1:7

Dear Lord,

Thank You for my sweet daughter. I pray You would give us time this week to connect. Inspire me to find creative ways of blessing my daughter. I pray she knows how much I love her and how much You love her. I pray my daughter would continue to mature in her relationship with You. Bless her with time spent in Your Word and prayer. I pray against the temptation to sin. Help my daughter to exercise self-control in all areas of her life. I pray she would be self-controlled in the habits she forms, in the desires she craves, in the ways she expresses herself, and in the words she chooses to share with others. I pray my daughter would have the strength to deny her flesh when it is craving more. I pray she is able to resist the temptation to sin. Help her to stay pure. I pray against the temptation of lust, especially with online pornography being so accessible. Help my daughter to restrain herself from curiously clicking on anything impure. Help her to stay healthy. I pray my daughter is self-disciplined. Give her the ability to structure her day that maximizes her time. Yet, I also pray she is flexible with her schedule for those spontaneous encounters You have for her to experience. Although I pray my daughter is self-controlled, I pray she would not be a controlling person. Help her to adjust easily to change. Holy Spirit, fill my daughter's heart and help her exercise self-control in all things so that You, Lord, may be glorified.

In Jesus' name, AMEN!

Don't

Listen

Don't listen to the enemy when he tries to convince you that you are failing as a parent. Don't let insecurity or doubt invade your heart. Be confident in your relationship with God in Christ Jesus and know that He is moving through you for an extraordinary purpose.

DAY 24

Protect Her

2 Thessalonians 3:3

Dear Lord,

I pray for my daughter right now. Please cover her with a hedge of protection. Guard her and keep her safe. There is so much evil in this world, and I know the enemy wants to destroy her. I pray against his attacks in Jesus' name. I pray You would anoint my daughter with Your peace. Fill her with Your strength. Comfort her with Your Word. I pray my daughter would apply the wisdom You have generously given to her so that she may live a long life. I pray the wisdom You have gifted to her keeps her away from dangerous situations. May Your Holy Spirit guide her throughout each day. Speak to her heart and train her to hear You, O God. Protect her heart and her mind from negativity. Protect her from people who don't have her interests in mind. Protect her from the violence, the sexual assaults, and the terrorism that is happening more frequently. I pray You would protect her from anyone who is seeking to take advantage of her. Foil their plans in Jesus' name. Protect my daughter from the chains of addiction. Protect her from choosing sin. Open her eyes so that she may see a way out from the temptation. Keep her safe and secure. If any trouble does reach my daughter, please give her the strength to persevere through it while maintaining her faith in You. Thank You for Your faithfulness and thank You for being her protector.

In Jesus' name, AMEN!

DAY 25

An Encourager

Proverbs 16:24

Dear Lord,

Thank You for my sweet daughter. She is bright and beautiful. She is lovely and kind. I am so blessed by my daughter. May You be glorified because of her life. I lift up my daughter to You today, and I ask that You would overwhelm her with Your peace. Send people her way to affirm her. May Your Words comfort her and teach her. I pray my daughter would know she is a wonderful encourager. Help my daughter embrace this gift You have given to her. Help her to cultivate this gift that it may grow. Use her words to bless others. Give her the right thing at the right time. May she never fear speaking with others, whether it is with one person or many at once, give her courage to speak Your truth into their lives. If there is a situation where You don't want her to speak, seal her lips and help her to have the self-control not to say a word. I pray others would know my daughter by the insightful and inspirational words she has to share. I pray she has a love for speaking and writing. Show her creative ways she can be an encouragement to others. Reveal to her the impact she has in the lives of those closest to her. I pray she continues to encourage people the rest of her life. Send people into her life as well, who will encourage her and point her heart toward You. Whether she is joyful and rejoicing or feeling low, may You use others to speak life into her heart, affirmation into her mind, and truth for her soul to be fed by.

In Jesus' name, AMEN!

DAY 26

Loving Family

John 13:34

Dear Lord,

I love my daughter. I pray I would have eyes to see where she is at emotionally and spiritually. Help me, O Lord, to get down to her level, to be compassionate toward her, and to encourage her. I pray I would make more time every day to hold my daughter close and to connect with her. Help me to invite her to participate in the things I do so she can learn practical skills, but also so we can have time to talk. I pray You would use me to share wisdom with my daughter. Give us time together to talk openly about what we are experiencing in life, that it might deepen our relationship. I pray my daughter feels wanted and loved. Thank You for blessing our family with her. Thank You for loving her and raising her up to be the woman You created her to be. Please continue to build up her character. Mold her and shape her to be more like You. I pray she appreciates her family. I pray she loves her family, respects her family, and serves her family joyfully. I pray my daughter is inspired to find ways to bless her family and cultivate all the different relationships she has. I pray she feels connected and accepted. I also pray we are a catalyst that initiates a desire in her heart to have a family of her own. Give her a desire to be a wife and mother. Give her a desire to leave a powerful legacy that brings glory to You. I pray my daughter has a heart full of love to give to her husband and children one day. May You be magnified because of her love for You.

In Jesus' name, AMEN!

CHALLENGE

- #6 -

Pray With Her

Cultivate a relationship with your daughter where prayer is a priority. Ask her how she is doing and offer to pray with her. You can even ask her to make a list for you as a guide to pray for her specific needs throughout the week.

DAY 17

Yieled To The Lord

James 4:7

Dear Lord,

You are so amazing. I come to You in prayer to lift up my daughter. May she feel Your presence all around her. May she be overwhelmed by Your peace. God, I pray my daughter is yielded to You. I pray she gives You her whole heart. I pray she never hides anything from You. I pray she never feels fear or shame. Shine Your light into her life. In a time when it is unpopular to follow You, I pray she doesn't conform to this world. I pray she never falls astray. Keep her in the palm of Your hands. Reveal to her why she should be yielded to You. Teach her how to be yielded to You. Please send people into her life who have incredible relationships with You who can guide her and encourage her in the faith. Please send her some mature women who can walk her through Your scripture, teaching her how to love others, specifically her husband and children. I pray these mentors would invest into my daughter and enjoy participating in her life. I pray against pride puffing up in my daughter's heart. Extinguish pride, O Lord. Keep it far from her. I pray my daughter's heart is humble and teachable. I pray she flees evil and resists the enemy. I pray against temptation that tries to snatch her from You. May she submit to You in all her ways. Wonderful Lord, please affirm her faith in You. Remind her every day of Your love for her. Remind her to walk in victory. Fill her heart with passion. Fill her heart with a desire to be intimate with You.

In Jesus' name, AMEN!

DAY 18

Her Friends

Proverbs 27:17

Dear Lord,

I pray for my daughter's friends. I pray she would be surrounded by people who love You. If she has friends that do not know You, please use her to influence them to turn their hearts toward You. I pray my daughter would choose friends who are respectful and who obey the law. I pray they seek to bless others and serve others. I pray they walk in righteousness and integrity. May the influence they have in my daughter's life be positive. Use them to point her heart toward You. I pray for my daughter's friend's families. Draw them closer to Yourself. I pray they are healthy people, who intentionally pursue You. I pray they guard the truth. I pray they would be willing to pray with my daughter and affirm her faith in You. I pray these families live with moral convictions, striving to live righteously. I pray my daughter and her friends do extraordinary things for Your Kingdom. May they inspire one another and spur each other on to do good works in Jesus' name. I pray they would keep each other accountable to reading Your Word every day. I pray they would not be idle. I pray they would not pursue selfish gain. I pray they would not be foolish. Holy Spirit, build up these friendships, so they last a lifetime. Bless my daughter's friendships with laughter, genuine love, compassion, and camaraderie.

In Jesus' name, AMEN!

DAY 29

Like Christ

1 Peter 2:21

Dear Lord,

Thank You for Jesus Christ. Thank You for His testimony and the example He has left for us to follow. I pray my daughter would know Your testimony. I pray she would desire to follow Your example. Transform her and make her like Christ. I pray my daughter is kind, compassionate, and forgiving. I pray she embraces people with love. May nothing ever hinder her from loving unconditionally. I pray she welcomes children and embraces them just like Jesus does. I pray she joyfully serves the needs of others. I pray she loves You, Lord, and that she recognizes You as her Heavenly Father. May she have a heart of prayer, petitioning for Your perfect will to be done on earth. May she seek time alone with You and read Your Word daily. May she walk humbly with You. I also pray she would be a person of integrity. When difficult or even painful circumstances happen, please help her to remember what Christ did for her when He went to the cross. I pray she is willing to sacrifice things that You ask her to sacrifice as she pursues Your will. If she endures persecution, may she endure it without losing her faith. May hope abound in her soul. I pray she is a woman who has incredible hope no matter what she experiences. I pray she never feels defeated, rather may she confidently live knowing You defeated death once and for all. I pray my daughter abides in You and follows in Your footsteps!

In Jesus' name, AMEN!

Love
your

family

Love your family by taking time to sit with them today. Listen to them, play with them, read to them, teach them, pray with them. You are not guaranteed tomorrow...so don't forsake the opportunities you have today to be with them and share God's love with them.

DAY 30
An Extraordinary life

John 10:10

Dear Lord,

Thank You for my daughter's life. I think it is incredible that You created her with purpose. May she value the gift of life You have gifted to her. I pray she sees every new day as an opportunity to tell others about how wonderful You are. I pray her heart is sensitive to where You are leading her. Give her courage to follow You and to carry out the work You have prepared for her to do. I pray my daughter has an extraordinary life. I pray she confidently knows You desire her to experience an abundant life. Help her to know You desire her to enjoy the loveliness of life. I pray she is able to identify her gifts and use them to build Your Kingdom. May she be eager to serve You in any capacity she can. Help her to have a vision and hope for her future. I pray my daughter sees the extraordinary in everyday life. Give her a perspective that is refreshing for her and others around her. May she turn hearts toward You because of the life she decides to live. Protect her from the enemy who seeks to destroy her life. Guard her against the terrible schemes of the evil one. May she be strong to endure any and every circumstance that comes her way. I pray the opportunities You give my daughter draw her closer to You. I pray my daughter would be eager to use the skills and talents You have blessed her with for Your Kingdom.

In Jesus' name, AMEN!

DAY 31

An Extraordinary Marriage

Ephesians 5:22-33

Dear Lord,

Your goodness and faithfulness are never-ending. I love You, Lord. Thank You for Your provision. Thank You for Your amazing grace. I lift up my daughter to You and petition for her future. I pray she continues to pursue an intimate relationship with You. May You reveal yourself to her in beautiful ways. Remind her of her purpose and the plans You have for her. May Your Holy Spirit guide her and may she be sensitive to hearing Your voice. Lead my daughter in the ways she should go. Give her confidence as she chooses to live for You. I pray she has a positive perspective of marriage. I pray she has a desire to get married if it is in Your will. May she understand why You created marriage and the purpose of marriage. I pray a blessing over my daughter's marriage. I pray her husband believes that Jesus Christ is Lord and Savior, confessing it with his mouth. I pray his family loves You and believes Your Word is truth. I pray he fears You, Lord. I pray he loves You and my daughter with all of his heart. May he lead her according to Your Word. I pray he cherishes my daughter and protects her heart in every way. I pray she respects him and loves him with her whole heart. May they embrace being one and may they glorify You with their relationship. I pray their marriage is a reflection of Your love for all. Use their marriage to draw others closer to Yourself. I pray they pursue intimacy with You and with each other. I pray they work together to serve others joyfully. I pray they experience an extraordinary marriage.

In Jesus' name, AMEN!

CHALLENGE

- #7 -

Her Future

Marriage is a wonderful gift to look forward to.
Invite your daughter to pray with you for her
future husband.

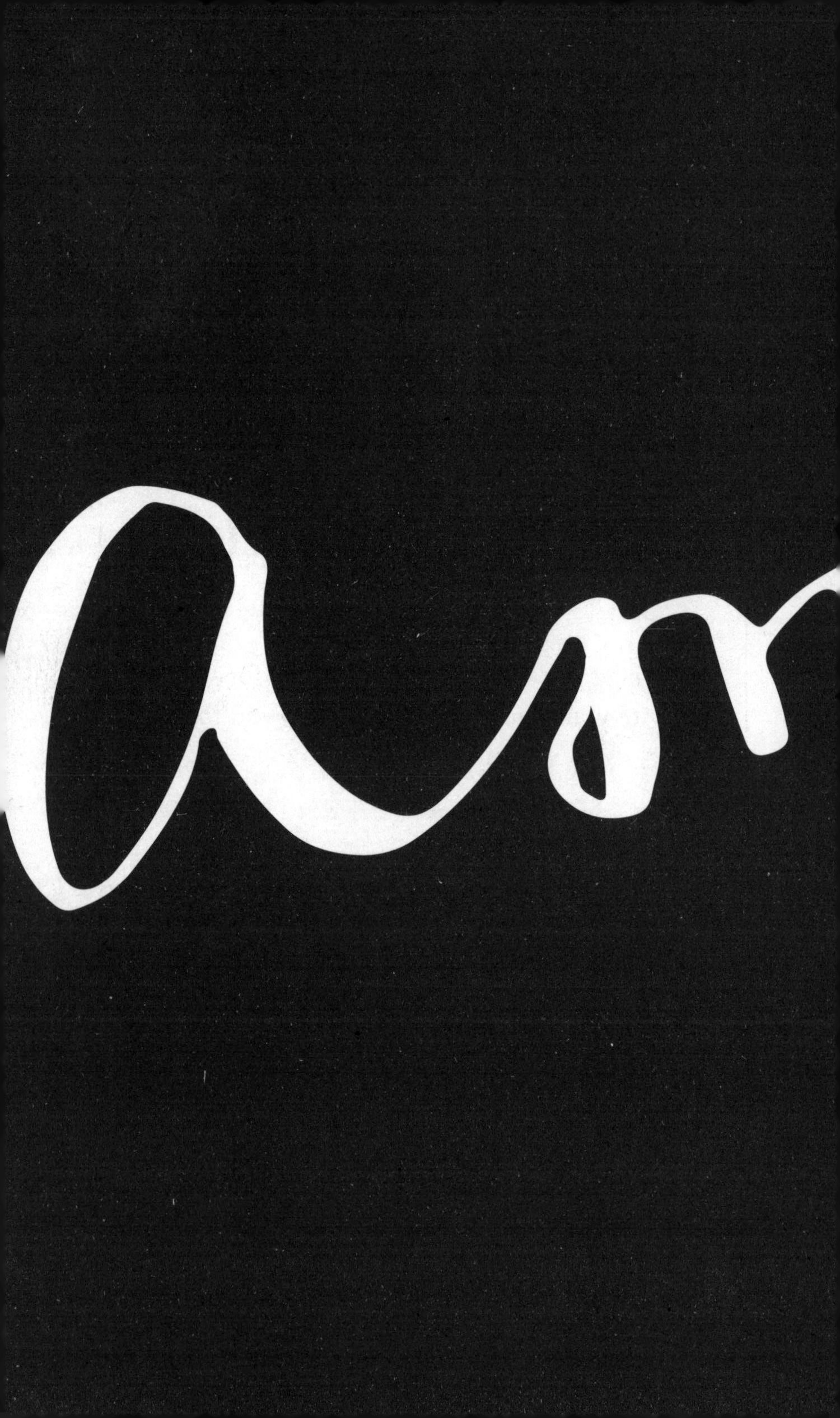

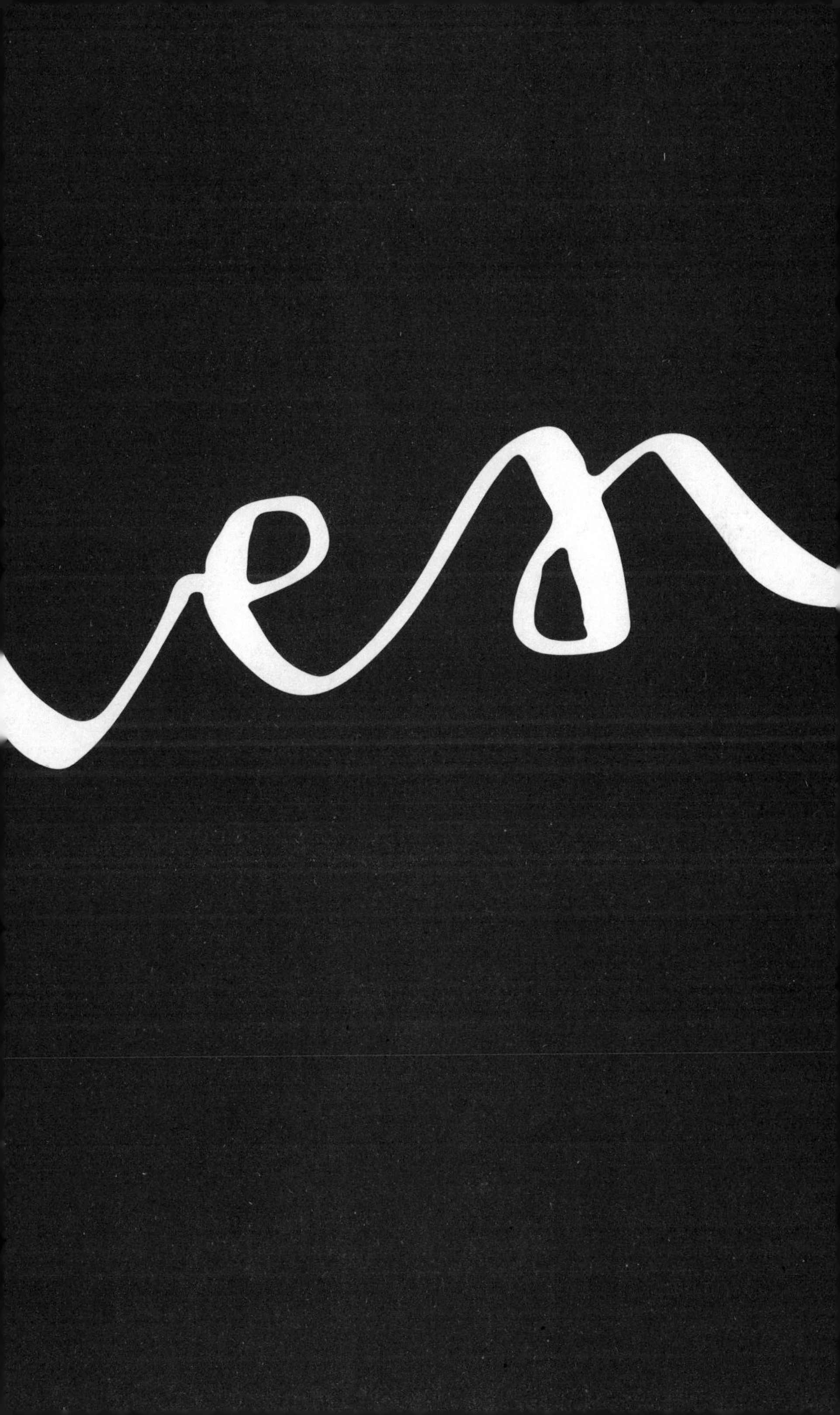

PRAY FOR YOUR MARRIAGE

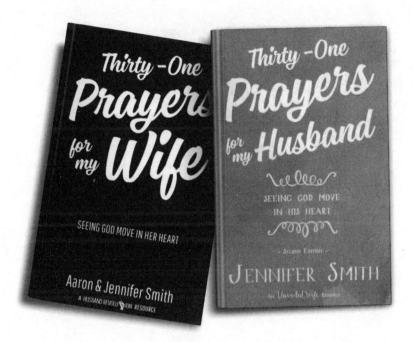

My husband and I wrote these two books to help inspire other couples to pray for each other. Grab this bundle and take the 31-day challenge to pray for each other.

Visit Our Store Today
Shop.unveiledwife.com

GROW CLOSER TO GOD & EACH OTHER

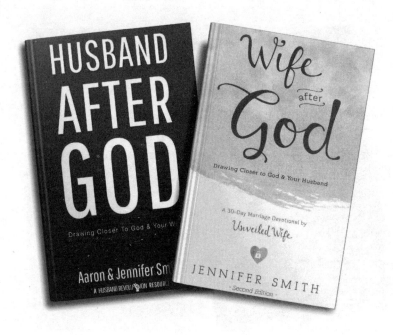

These two complementary resources walk through important biblical marriage principles, while also addressing different areas of life that a husband and wife might struggle with.

Visit Our Store Today
Shop.unveiledwife.com

GREAT GIFT IDEA FOR SINGLES & ENGAGED

These are great resources to help teenagers purpose their hearts for what God has for their future marriage or anyone else who feels strongly about getting married and cares for the heart of their future spouse.

Visit Our Store Today
Shop.unveiledwife.com

FRAMEABLE ART

Praying for your daughter is a beautiful way of loving her. Be reminded of the time you have spent praying for her and be reminded to continue praying for her with this detailed watercolor print of the lily from the cover of this book.

When we decided to make "The Lily" print for you, we envisioned it hanging in your daughter's nursery or bedroom as a thoughtful reminder for her and for you that she is being prayed for!

You can order a full color print in 5 x 7 or an 8 x 10 available only at our online store:

Shop.unveiledwife.com/prints

If this prayer book has impacted your faith please let me know by posting a testimony here:
31prayersformydaughter.com

For more marriage and family resources please visit:
shop.unveiledwife.com

Sign-up for daily prayers by email:
unveiledwife.com/daily-prayer/
husbandrevolution.com/daily-prayer/

Get connected:
Facebook.com/unveiledwife
Instagram.com/unveiledwife

Facebook.com/husbandrevolution
Instagram.com/husbandrevolution